The Story of the Garden of Eden

Patricia A. Pingry

Illustrated by Teresa B. Ragland

A Word to Parents and Friends

This story is one of a series of biblical stories especially written, illustrated, and designed to explain a difficult concept in a gentle and simple manner.

Even the youngest child will understand the timeless lesson inherent in each Bible story. Most of all, preschoolers, beginning readers, and older children will enjoy hearing and reading these exciting accounts of heroes from one of the oldest and most exciting books of all: the Holy Bible.

Ideals Children's Books
Nashville, Tennessee

Copyright © 1994 by Hambleton-Hill Publishing, Inc.
Published by Ideals Children's Books
An imprint of Hambleton-Hill Publishing, Inc.
Nashville, Tennessee 37218

ISBN 0-8249-8654-7

Long ago there was a beautiful garden just east of a place called Eden. A river flowed out of Eden, watered this garden, then split into four rivers. The land around the rivers contained gold, onyx, and precious gems. God had made this garden as the home for the first two people on earth.

God had made everything—the sun, the moon, the stars, the oceans, the earth, the trees, the grass, the flowers, the fish, the birds, and the Garden of Eden.

God created everything in six days. He said, "Let there be light," and there was light.

God said, "Let there be land and let there be waters."

God said, "Let there be grass and trees."

God said, "Let there be the sun and the moon and stars and winter and summer."

God said, "Let there be whales and fishes and birds."

And all this took five days.

On the next day, the sixth day, God made cattle and panthers and worms. He then took some dirt and formed a man, much as a sculptor might fashion a statue. But God breathed life into the man and He named the man Adam. He set Adam right in the middle of the Garden.

There was every kind of tree and plant imaginable in the Garden.
There were peach trees, apple trees, and banana trees. There were
grapevines with the sweetest and largest red, white, and purple
grapes. There were blackberry, raspberry, and blueberry bushes.
There were huge roses of all colors and daisies and hibiscus and
hollyhocks. When Adam was hungry, he had only to walk around
and pick fruit off a tree or berries from a bush and eat. There
were no thorns on these berry bushes and no thorns on the roses.
There was nothing in the Garden to prick or hurt Adam.

Adam could do anything he wanted to do in the Garden—except one thing. God gave Adam only one rule. In the middle of the Garden stood a tree.

God said to Adam, "This is the Tree of Knowledge. This is my tree and you are to leave it alone."

God made the punishment very hard. "If you eat fruit from this tree, you will die."

God brought all the animals he had made to Adam who named each of them. Adam had a lot of fun naming lions, tigers, gnus, anteaters, lynxes, orangutans, and platypuses. God then brought the birds to Adam who named them eagles, turkeys, owls, penguins, emus, ostriches, and kiwis.

Adam could do anything he wanted in the Garden.
He could run with the deer and antelope or ride on the
backs of lions. He could squeeze fresh juice right into
his mouth. Adam could eat rutabagas for breakfast or
watermelons at midnight.

Each day the sun shone in the Garden and each night a heavy
mist rose from the ground and refreshed the trees and flowers. It
never rained or snowed, and no weeds grew in the Garden of
Eden. At dusk, God walked in the Garden and talked with Adam.

God decided to give Adam a gift. He would give Adam someone who was like himself, yet different. God would give Adam a companion. While Adam was sleeping, God removed a bone from Adam's side and created another person. When Adam awoke, God brought the new person to Adam for a name. Adam named the person "Woman."

In the Garden, there was a brightly colored serpent. This snake did not slide along on its belly, but moved upright. It wasn't even a snake at all, but was the evil Satan disguised as a snake. One day the serpent spoke to the woman as she and Adam were walking in the Garden.

"Has God told you that you may eat of every tree in the Garden?" asked the serpent.

The woman answered, "No, there is one tree that we must not eat of and cannot touch. If we eat its fruit, we will die."

"You won't die," the serpent exclaimed. "The fruit is so good—it will make you smarter. You will know all that God knows, that's all. Go ahead and try it. Just try one bite and see what it's like. One bite won't hurt."

The woman looked at the tree. "I would like to be smarter. The fruit looks good. What harm is there in one bite?"

She reached up and broke off one piece of fruit. She took a bite. The serpent was right. It was delicious! She offered Adam a bite.

Now Adam remembered what God had said. But the woman was eating the fruit. She had not dropped down dead. If she could eat it, he could too! So Adam took a bite.

Suddenly, the woman looked at Adam. He had no clothes on! And
she had no clothes on either! The woman ran behind a bush. Then
Adam, too, realized they were both naked. He broke off a branch
and covered himself with it. Then he tied some leaves together for
the woman to use to cover herself.

Just then, they heard the Lord God walking in the Garden. Dusk was falling and mist would soon be rising. It was the time of day when Adam and the Lord God walked together and named the animals and talked.

"Adam, where are you?" called the Lord God. "Why are you hiding? Come here."

Adam crept out from the bushes and stood before God. "I was hiding because I did not have any clothes on. I was ashamed that I was naked."

"Who told you that you were naked?" demanded the Lord God. Now God knew instantly what had happened, but He asked, "Did you eat the fruit that I told you not to eat?"

"I did," Adam whimpered, "but it was not my fault. The woman gave it to me. I only ate it because she did."

God turned to the woman, "What do you have to say?"

"It's not my fault," she whined. "The serpent told me that it would be good to eat. He told me that we would not die."

Then God turned to the serpent, "You lied. And from now on you will be the most hated of all creatures. You will eat dust and you will crawl on your belly forevermore. There will come a day when you, Satan, will be destroyed."

Then God turned to Adam and the woman. He sounded disappointed as He said, "You will know pain and you will have to work hard for your food and your home. Because you disobeyed me, all the earth is changed. Plants will now grow thorns and prickles. Plants will come up, but they will also die. Animals will kill each other for food and homes. And one day, you too will die, just as I said."

God then gave Adam and the woman coats of skins to wear, and He drove them out of the Garden of Eden. God commanded cherubim with flaming swords to guard the entrance to the Garden so that no one may ever enter again.

And Adam and the woman, whom Adam named Eve, plowed the land and planted crops and built their own house. They killed animals for food and clothing and grew tired at the end of each day.

But sometimes, just as dusk was falling, they thought about a time they could scarcely remember when they walked in the cool of the evening and spoke with God.